Pebble

I DON'T BULLY

I Am
Responsible

WITHDRAWN

by Melissa Higgins

Consulting Editor: Gail Saunders-Smith, PhD

Content Consultant: Susan M. Swearer, PhD
Professor of School Psychology and Licensed
Psychologist; Co-Director, Bullying Research Network
University of Nebraska–Lincoln

CAPSTONE PRESS
a capstone imprint

Pebble Books are published by Capstone Press,
1710 Roe Crest Drive, North Mankato, Minnesota 56003
www.capstonepub.com

Library of Congress Cataloging-in-Publication Data
Higgins, Melissa, 1953–
I am responsible / by Melissa Higgins.
pages cm.—(Pebble books. I don't bully)
Summary: "Simple text and full color photographs describe how to be responsible,
not a bully"—Provided by publisher.
Includes bibliographical references and index.
Audience: Age 5–8.
Audience: K to grade 3.
ISBN 978-1-4765-4068-9 (library binding)
ISBN 978-1-4765-5172-2 (paperback)
ISBN ISBN 978-1-4765-6037-3 (ebook pdf)
1. Respect—Juvenile literature. I. Title.
BJ1451.H54 2014
179'.9—dc23   2013029993

Note to Parents and Teachers

The I Don't Bully set supports national curriculum standards
for social studies related to people and cultures. This book
describes being responsible. The images support early
readers in understanding the text. The repetition of words
and phrases helps early readers learn new words. This book
also introduces early readers to subject-specific vocabulary
words, which are defined in the Glossary section. Early
readers may need assistance to read some words and to use
the Table of Contents, Glossary, Read More, Internet Sites,
and Index sections of the book.

Printed in the United States of America in North Mankato, Minnesota.
092013   007764CGS14

Table of Contents

4

I Do My Part

I do what I'm supposed to do. I'm responsible. I don't bully!

I only take credit
for my own work.
Kids who bully
brag about things
they haven't done.

I admit when I make
a mistake. Kids who bully
blame other people
for their mistakes.

OFFICE

I do my part
to stop bullying.
If someone is being
teased, I say it's
not funny.

I Work Hard

I prepare and do
the best job I can.
Kids who bully
make others do
their work.

When my work is hard,
I keep trying.
Kids who bully
make fun of kids
who try hard.

I Am In Charge of Me

I think about what
will happen before I act.
Kids who bully lose control.
They don't care who
gets hurt.

I'm patient.
Kids who bully
get angry if they
have to wait.

I Make Good Choices

The choices I make matter.

I choose not to be a bully!

Glossary

admit—to agree that something is true

blame—to hold yourself or someone else responsible for something that happened

brag—telling someone something to show off

bully—to be mean to someone else over and over again

choice—picking from several things

credit—praise

patient—able to wait

prepare—to get ready

responsible—choosing to do what you are supposed to do

Read More

Marshall, Shelley. *Molly the Great's Messy Bed: A Book about Responsibility.* Character Education with Super Ben and Molly the Great. Berkeley Heights, N.J.: Enslow Publishers, 2010.

Mayer, Cassie. *Being Responsible.* Citizenship. Chicago: Heinemann Library, 2008.

National, Walt. *I Am Responsible.* Kids of Character. New York: Gareth Stevens Pub., 2011.

Internet Sites

FactHound offers a safe, fun way to find Internet sites related to this book. All of the sites on FactHound have been researched by our staff.

Here's all you do:

Visit *www.facthound.com*

Type in this code: 9781476540689

Index

Word Count: 142
Grade: 1
Early-Intervention Level: 13

Editorial Credits
Jeni Wittrock, editor; Juliette Peters, designer; Svetlana Zhurkin, media researcher;
Kathy McColley, production specialist; Sarah Schuette, photo stylist;
Marcy Morin, photo scheduler

Photo Credits
Capstone Studio/Karon Dubke